...of Wales

...son
...is of Wales
...rents,
and The Duke of Edinburgh,
and great grandmother
H M The Queen Mother

HM Queen Elizabeth II

Born	*21st April 1926*
Marriage	*20th November 1947*
Coronation	*2nd June 1953*
Silver Jubilee	*1977*
Family	*Prince Charles born 1948*
	Princess Anne born 1950
	Prince Andrew born 1960
	Prince Edward born 1964

Acknowledgments:

The author and publishers wish to acknowledge the use of photographs as follows:

B B C Hulton Picture Library, pages 18, 48; Camera Press Ltd, cover and pages 37 (top), 42 (middle), 43, 49; Central Press Photos, page 8; Colour Library International Ltd, pages 9 (left), 24, 31, 39; Fox Photos Ltd, pages 21, 22, 25, 30, 35 (top), 36; Tim Graham, pages 27 (top), 45 (middle), 50; Imperial War Museum, pages 20, 42 (top); Keystone Press Agency Ltd, pages 4, 9 (right), 12, 13, 14, 15 (top), 16, 19, 32 (top), 46; National Portrait Gallery, pages 6, 7, 10; Popperfoto, pages 17, 23; Rex Features, page 38 (bottom); John Scott, pages 5, 15 (bottom), 26, 27 (bottom), 28, 29, 32 (bottom), 33, 34, 35 (bottom), 38 (top pictures), 40, 41, 44, 45 (bottom, and right), 47 and back cover; Syndication International Ltd, fep and page 37 (bottom).

The family tree on the back endpaper is by R M Powell, the drawings on page 11 are by Drury Lane Studios, and the drawing on page 51 is by Ian Rawlings.

First edition

Her Majesty
The Queen

by IAN A MORRISON MA PhD

Ladybird Books Loughborough

'Treetops' in Kenya where Princess Elizabeth was staying when she became Queen

"For the first time in the history of the world a young girl climbed into a tree one day a Princess . . . and climbed down from the tree the next day a Queen — God bless her."

The old man who wrote this had freed villagers from man-eating leopards and tigers, by tracking them down single-handed through jungles and over mountains. But he wasn't some shadowy hero from an ancient epic, and what he wrote about the Princess was no medieval fairy tale either.

Those were the words Jim Corbett entered in the log-book of a hut built in the upper branches of a giant ficus tree, which overlooked a clearing in the forests of Africa. The tree stood in a wild-life sanctuary near Nyeri in Kenya. The year was 1952, and Princess Elizabeth had come with her husband Philip to spend 5th and 6th February there, watching rhinos and elephants. It was on that moonlit spring night that she inherited the throne.

Somehow, things still happen to our Royal Family in ways that bring the magic of fairy tales into the 20th century . . .

And today, the Queen still enjoys going on safari

5

Princess Elizabeth had become a Queen who would rule as Sovereign in her own right. It was *her* father, not Philip's, who had been King George VI. Because of this, though Philip was her husband, he would always remain her Consort, and he would not become a king himself. The next King was likely to be their son, Prince Charles, so he became known as 'the Heir Apparent', though he was only three years old when his mother became Queen.

Most of the queens who have reigned as sole sovereign have been memorable ladies: from Boudicca in ancient times, through Mary Queen of

Queen Elizabeth I

Queen Anne and the Duke of Gloucester

Scots and the first Queen Elizabeth of England in the 16th century, to Queen Anne in the 18th, and then Queen Victoria in the 19th century.

In the long view of British history such Queens have been much rarer than Kings, but over the last two centuries that pattern has changed. With Victoria reigning right through from 1837 until 1901, and then Queen Elizabeth being on the throne from 1952, Britain has been ruled by Queens for almost twice as long as by Kings in the years since Victoria was crowned.

Queen Victoria

Queen Elizabeth II

Princess Elizabeth was twenty-five when the news came that she was Queen. Although she was older than Victoria had been when *she* became Queen, it must still have been hard to take on her new public role, while coping with her private grief over the death of her father. He had been ill for some time, but he had gone with her to Heathrow airport to see her off. And from the way she had enjoyed watching the animals that night, Jim Corbett was sure that the tragedy was unexpected.

The last wave from her father

She can have had little sleep the next night either, for by then she was airborne on the long journey back to London. Even after flying over six thousand kilometres, she had no chance of rest or privacy. Prime Ministers past and present were waiting to greet their new Queen as she came down the steps of the aircraft. In the days that followed, she had to take the main part in the ceremonies as her father lay in state at Westminster Hall, and then at his funeral at Windsor.

Almost a third of a million people filed past the coffin to show their liking for George VI, and their respect for the way that he had taken up the task of Kingship when it was thrust upon him so abruptly in his forties. He had grown up not expecting to be King. Although the throne came to his daughter with unwelcome suddenness, at least she had known since she was ten that she was likely to become Queen one day.

George VI lying in state   *Three Queens grieve*   9

George V

Although it became *likely* when she was ten that she would become Queen, it was not certain. As a girl, she had only become what was called 'Heir Presumptive'. This meant that if a royal son had been born, he would have taken over the line to the throne. The then Lady Airlie said that young Elizabeth used to say prayers for a little brother who would replace her as 'Heir Apparent'.

All this happened when she was ten, because it was then that her father became King. That year 1936 was an extraordinary one for the Royal Family.

his oldest son succeeded him as Edward VIII, as expected. But in the face of bitter controversy over his choice of a wife, he gave up the throne. On Friday 11th December his younger brother, Elizabeth's father, became King George VI, and the lives of her whole family changed.

It was the first time since the Wars of the Roses in 1483 that there had been three kings on the throne of England within twelve months, and the time before that had been back in 1066, with the coming of William the Conqueror.

When Elizabeth's grandfather King George V died in January 1936,

George VI

*Queen Mary
with her grand-daughter*

A happy princess on her tricycle

The unexpectedness of it all even comes out in her names. Queen Victoria had wished that all girl children close to the line of succession should include 'Victoria' amongst their names. Her grandfather King George V however had agreed with Elizabeth's parents that this was quite unnecessary for her. So she was christened Elizabeth Alexandra Mary, though at first Lilibet was what she called herself. Nicknames came as naturally to the Royal Family as to ordinary families. When she was four she decided to call her newly arrived sister 'Bud' . . . telling Lady Cynthia Asquith they shouldn't call just a baby 'Margaret *Rose*'.

Lady Cynthia was with the children the day their father became King, and she tells how Elizabeth found a letter on the hall table addressed to 'Her Majesty the Queen'. The young princess asked, "That's *Mummy* now, isn't it?"

Not suspecting that they might ascend the throne one day, her parents had set out

Driving with her Grandfather

to avoid the stiffness of the old Royal court in which her father had grown up. Treasuring privacy, they had tried instead to bring up the girls in the more relaxed style of her mother's people, the Bowes-Lyons.

A family outing

Since her father had been born a Prince, the 'public' side of Elizabeth's life started even before he became King. When she was quite tiny, she had to begin to get used to appearing with her parents on official occasions, since they were the Duke and Duchess of York.

The Coronation of George VI, 1937

Her grandmother, Queen Mary, seems to have felt that when you are small there is a very narrow line between getting over your shyness and becoming a show-off. Once, at the Queen's Hall, she had Lilibet taken out by a back way and sent home by taxi, so that she would not get the cheers she hoped for from the people out front . . . But by the time the Princess was eight, Lady Colville recalls that as leading bridesmaid at a Royal wedding she not only knew how to behave with dignity herself, but kept her little sister in order as well!

At their parents' Coronation too, she kept an eye on Margaret, though as she said afterwards, she only had to give her a nudge once or twice . . . We don't know whether Queen Mary was pleased or not when a sound-meter in Whitehall showed that the carriage taking her home with her grand-daughters got even louder cheers than their newly crowned parents!

The new King and Queen with their daughters, in Coronation robes

In 1941 – 'School' at Windsor Castle

No sooner had the family begun to grow into its new Royal role than the Second World War broke out. Evacuating the girls to safety overseas was discussed. But as their mother put it, "The children won't leave without me; I won't leave without the King; and the King will never leave . . ."

Buckingham Palace was bombed while the King and Queen were in it. The Princesses were thought to be safer at Windsor Castle, but there were risks there too. Not all were due to the enemy: a naval pilot (who survived the war to become a Lord) recently admitted he lost control of a Swordfish biplane while doing "unofficial" aerobatics over the Castle, and very nearly came spinning through their roof at 60 metres a second . . .

When the war started, Elizabeth was a child, but when it ended, she was a young woman of nineteen. She had known the deaths of an uncle and family friends, just as her father and mother had lost friends and relatives in the First World War. It had been a grim time to be growing up, and when his daughters went out to mingle in the peace celebrations around the Palace, George VI wrote in his diary, "Poor darlings, they have never had any fun yet."

In uniform again — this time the ATS

In 1939 — just before the War began — Princess Elizabeth had met a young Naval cadet at Dartmouth, called Philip. She was then only thirteen, but he was eighteen, so he went to sea on active service, just as her father had done in the First World War. And like her father, who served in *HMS Collingwood* in the Battle of Jutland, he did well in action. He was mentioned in dispatches for his initiative, manning searchlights on *HMS Valiant* in the night fight off Cape Matapan. *Valiant* was damaged, but they sank two enemy cruisers.

HMS Valiant

Matapan is in Greece, an appropriate place for the young naval officer, because though his family is of Danish blood, he was then Prince Philip of Greece. He had however gone to school at Gordonstoun in Scotland, and as a nephew of Lord Louis Mountbatten, he was in touch with the British Royal Household.

Throughout the war he wrote to the Princess, and visited the family on his leave from the Navy. The King came to like him, but everything had to wait

The engagement photograph

until the fighting was over. In 1946 they decided to get married, and on 10th July 1947 their engagement was officially announced from Buckingham Palace.

21

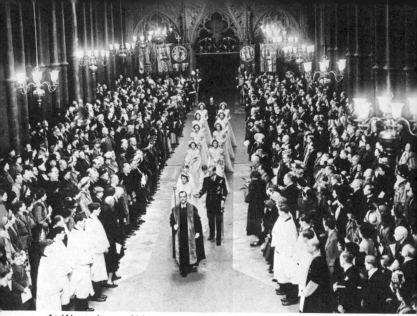

At Westminster Abbey

The wedding group

As Britain's old wartime leader Winston Churchill put it, the engagement came as a flash of colour in a grey world. Though the fighting was over, Britain had only survived at a cost. But now a Royal Wedding to a young Navy man offered the chance of a bright national celebration that many people could identify with, in a quite personal way. With the young men home from the war, marriages were in the minds of many other families.

It has been said that since a princely marriage is a brilliant edition of something universally shared, "it rivets mankind." That statement was made in Victorian times, but as the wedding of Charles and Diana shows, it still rings true towards the end of the 20th century.

In the post-war situation of 1947, food and clothing were still rationed, yet hundreds of girls sent the Princess presents of the newly-fashionable nylon stockings, though these were difficult for them to get for themselves. The very fact of shortages and drabness made people keen that the wedding of Elizabeth and Philip should be carried off with the brilliance traditional to our Royal weddings, for everyone to enjoy.

Dated *Twenty second day of September* 1947

Licence for the Marriage

of

Her Royal Highness The
Princess *Elizabeth Alexandra Mary*
with
Lieutenant *Philip Mountbatten, R.N.*

The marriage licence

23

Even the attention the wedding attracted around the globe was outshone by the interest shown in the Queen's Coronation five years later, on 2nd June 1953. Nearly a quarter of the world's population was still linked with the Commonwealth then, and even the people of America and France, who had cast off monarchy centuries before, queued to see colour films of the pageantry. Television was new in many British homes, so this was the first Coronation when so many could share the events as they actually happened.

Coronation 2nd June 1953

Seated in the 13th century Coronation Chair

The day started well, with the news that a Commonwealth team had made the first ascent of Mount Everest. Then stage by stage, the processions and fanfares built up to the consecration and crowning in Westminster Abbey. That was a solemn moment symbolic of the responsibility of representing a nation, to itself and to the world. Then the new Queen went out to meet her people, and the day's celebrations got underway.

Her children, Prince Charles and Princess Anne, joined her on the balcony of Buckingham Palace, just as she had joined her parents after *their* Coronation. But little Charles didn't match her 1937 gift: her own account of the events, written in red in a school jotter —
"To Mummy and Papa. In Memory of Their Coronation, From Lilibet By Herself."

The Duke of Edinburgh in ducal coronet

At the Fiji Islands, in 1977

The overseas interest in the Queen has continued ever since Coronation day. Because her position is independent of party politics, she has been able to act as a very special ambassador for the British people, and also to help to sustain the links between the very different nations of the Commonwealth. She emphasises that to her the Crown is not just an abstract symbol of unity, but that the Royal Family is a personal and living bond shared between the Commonwealth peoples.

She has led goodwill visits to over a hundred countries, scattered across the continents from tropical forests to arctic snows. Sometimes she has

*At Tuvalu, in the Pacific Ocean, in 1982
— the Queen is rowed in a canoe*

met people in huge crowds, sometimes as individuals, in all kinds of situations from opera houses to leper camps. Indeed, over the last thirty years she has journeyed farther than any previous sovereign in British history.

Although the air age has made this possible, she has travelled by sea too, as well as by road and rail. And however she goes, each royal visit needs painstaking organisation by her staff, and also demands a lot of stamina from her.

At Riyadh, Saudi Arabia, in 1979

A Guide camp at Windsor

Opening Parliament

Within Britain, her work has extraordinary variety as well. One day she may be presenting Sunday school prizes at Sandringham, the next welcoming a foreign head of state. At either event people would be disappointed in her if she did not seem well informed, and interested. To live up to what is expected of a Queen, occasions great and small have to be carried through equally well. A talent for simplicity rather than ceremonial is needed if a visit is to please children or old people in hospital, yet the complicated rituals of the great state events have to go off with flying colours *every* time.

These state occasions involve something deeper than vivid theatre to draw rich tourists from abroad (though they certainly do that). They remind the British themselves of the historical roots that bind the nation together, and the Queen has become known for keeping an expert eye on their details. But as Prince Philip once put it, when you're rowing a boat you are in for trouble if you just look where you've been... so although the Queen is a guardian of the nation's living past, she also sees it as part of her job to encourage modern industry and enterprise, through such schemes as The Queen's Awards for Export Achievement and Technological Achievement.

Trooping the Colour

The expertness that people assume will be shown in handling all these different kinds of activities isn't something that 'just happens' from the day you become a Queen. Behind every public engagement in Britain and overseas, there lies a great deal of personal homework, as well as the checking of practical details with her staff. And by no means all her work is done in the public eye. There is a lot of office-work in most of her days, with administration and correspondence arising from the charities and organisations with which she is associated, and from the running of the Royal households and estates, as well as her constitutional duties.

As Prime Ministers of all parties have found out, she takes a caring interest in the state papers submitted to her each day. The very fact that the Monarchy in Britain stands aside from any party political ambitions can give special value to her traditional weekly consultation with the Prime Minister. As Harold Wilson once said, the Queen was the one working colleague to whom he could take national problems, without feeling he was sharpening a knife for his own back.

One of the State despatch boxes

The Queen at her desk in February 1982

Riding with her father

As a young princess, it seems that she said that if ever she was Queen, she would make a law that horses deserved Sunday as a day off. As Queen, the compliment has been returned by the horses. They have given her relaxation, and helped her to keep fit to carry out her taxing range of duties.

We tend to associate horses more with other members of the Royal Family. There is the Queen Mother for example, smuggling her Shetland pony indoors as a child, then still enjoying the races in her old age; Prince Philip with polo

Patting a Shetland pony

A quiet ride at Windsor

and carriage driving; Prince Charles enjoying polo
too, and trying his hand as a jockey; and of course
Princess Anne, whose riding is of Olympic standard.
But when Princess Elizabeth was small, she not only
had a collection of thirty toy horses, she got her first
real pony when she was just three years old. She has
been a horsewoman ever since, riding hard and
regularly, though in private and not in competition.
The public is thus much less aware of the Queen as
a keen rider than as a horse breeder, for jockeys
wearing her colours are often seen racing horses from
the royal racing stables.

Riding with President Reagan

33

The sport of Queens...

Royal racing stables go back to when the Crowns of England and Scotland were joined. Since James VI went to London to succeed the first Queen Elizabeth in 1603, sovereigns have spent most of their time in the south of their United Kingdom. But the Scottish connection involves more than colourful official events.

Balmoral — a favourite holiday home for the Royal Family from the time of Queen Victoria

Ever since Queen Victoria made Balmoral her special sanctuary, and particularly since the Queen Mother grew up at Glamis, the royal Scottish homes have been favourite family places. Though pressmen with telephoto lenses do try to stalk them through the heather, each generation

Prince Andrew takes the Corgis on holiday

has found privacy there. Prince Andrew claims his big brother keeps dozing off at Balmoral — and that Mother has to prod him regularly . . .

There is less scope for snoozing at Gordonstoun, Prince Philip's old school. The Queen sent her sons there, despite her husband's cheery view that only a Scotsman can really survive a Scottish Education!

Relaxing at Balmoral

The Investiture at Caernarvon Castle

The link of the Royal Family with Scotland had been emphasised when Prince Philip was made Duke of Edinburgh on the day that he married Princess Elizabeth. For generations, the link of the throne with Wales has been underlined by making the eldest son of the monarch Prince of Wales. As Queen, Elizabeth decided to follow that tradition. Charles was nine when she announced this, but she chose not to install him until he was fully grown and had studied the language and culture of the country. In the past, many who received the title had earned the dislike of the Welsh by the scant interest they showed in the Principality. Charles worked intensively at the

University of Aberystwyth to overcome this, and by the time the Queen presented him to the people of Wales at his Investiture at Caernarvon Castle in 1969, opinion polls showed that 90% were in favour of the Ceremony. Although extreme Nationalists certainly still disapprove, the enthusiasm with which the Princess of Wales and little Prince William of Wales have been greeted tells its own story.

A relaxed moment after the Investiture

The Investiture was memorable, but the Prince may have preferred to forget some of the souvenirs: you could stand or sit on him, dry dishes on him, or drink out of him . . . and he narrowly avoided being extruded as Welsh humbug rock . . .

The Prince of Wales, with his wife and baby son, arrives in Alice Springs, Australia, 1983

In Kuwait

Visiting New Zealand

While great occasions like the Investiture may catch our imagination, to a lot of people the real magic of majesty still lies in the prospect of actually meeting a member of the Royal Family as an individual . . . or at least coming near to it. Surveys suggest that of all world personalities, Queen Elizabeth is the one most dreamed about. But most of the dreams are not about the grandeur of public appearances: they are about having tea with her . . . It is a remarkable achievement for her to have struck a balance

In Canada, 1983

A walk-about at St Paul's in London during the Silver Jubilee

between two images that seem so different —
a glittering public figurehead for the nation, and
a private person with whom to enjoy a quiet
moment.

The figurehead role was one that earlier monarchs
were used to carrying out. The effort the present
Royal Family has put into making more personal
contacts has been one
of the main trends
characteristic of the
Queen's reign.
Methods such as
'walk-abouts' help
the Royal Family to
meet people away from
formal events, in
town and country
all over the world.

*A walk-about
in Melbourne, Australia*

Driving in an open carriage

Walk-abouts are well liked, because they let more people get close to the Queen. But not all may be well-wishers. Risk is a regrettably routine part of life in the public eye at her level. Earl Mountbatten was murdered during her reign, and the Pope and presidents of several countries have been shot by political extremists or the mentally unbalanced.

She is vulnerable when people crowd round during a walk-about; or when she is isolated in front of a huge crowd (as when she was riding to Trooping the Colour in 1981, and a pistol was fired at her. Happily it was loaded with blanks.) One would think that she might sleep safely at home, but in 1982 an intruder even got into her bedroom in Buckingham Palace. This was not the first time that something like that had happened. Her mother and oldest son have also shown steady nerves in coping with intrusions by night.

As her parents' decision to stay on in London during the bombing showed, it is in the family tradition to accept risks in their role as symbolic leaders of the nation. Today, no less than in the past, simple courage is a necessary quality in Royalty.

Preparing to Troop the Colour

HMS Kelly

Some celebrities seem to court danger just 'for kicks', or to draw attention to themselves. From time to time those who are against the whole idea of Royalty attack their sporting activities along those lines, and dismiss them as people who just indulge in risks in playboy style.

Admiral the Earl Mountbatten of Burma

To many however it has been the willingness of the Queen's family to accept real danger alongside their people whenever necessary that goes a long way towards explaining why they have kept the respect and affection of the British throughout the troubled 20th century. Uncles of the Queen died in the trenches in the First World War, and in the air in the Second. Several generations of her relatives have served under fire in the Navy. As we have seen, her father and husband saw action in the battles of Jutland and Matapan. During World War II, Lord Louis Mountbatten managed to save *HMS Kelly* despite battle damage in the North Sea, but then he had his destroyer sunk under him in the Mediterranean. In 1982, flying as a naval helicopter pilot, her son Prince Andrew took his turn as missile decoy off the Falklands.

Prince Andrew serving as a helicopter pilot

Prince Philip on active service

In a carriage driving competition

As Consort but not King, Prince Philip has been free to take rather more risks than the country feels their Sovereign should be exposed to . . . and not just of the serious physical kind. He hasn't had to avoid the risk of controversy as the Queen has done. The hundred and fifty or so speeches he makes each year give him plenty of openings for pithy comments, and inevitably not all of these please everybody. *Dontopedalogy* he says is the science of opening your mouth and putting your foot in it . . .

By grasping the opportunities of this greater freedom, he has been able to develop a much livelier style than was ever open to the last two kings, George V and VI. And whereas George V had felt that it was his duty to have Royal children brought up in what has been unkindly described as a tradition of unrelieved starchiness, Prince Philip has opened up the scope for his sons and daughter to emerge as characters with a touch of salt in their own right. The combination of this cheerful irascibility with the secure (indeed, serene) family image represented by the Queen and the Queen Mother, is one that has gone down well in Britain, and beyond. As a village banner put it during a Commonwealth tour: "GOD SAVE THE QUEEN – AND PLEASE KEEP AN EYE ON PRINCE PHILIP."

Refereeing a polo match

Formal for the races

At the helm

Prince Philip has remarked on the relief to parents when they find they have actually brought up a reasonable and civilised human being . . . and he and the Queen have clearly felt that raising a family is an important side of life (even as a little girl she had wanted "lots of cows, horses and children").

They tried to give their children privacy to develop naturally, while gradually introducing them to public duties, just as the Queen's own parents had done. Like her mother too, the Queen made time to start their education, teaching them their alphabet herself. Then, with her aim of a 20th century monarchy closer to the people, she sent them out to school, instead of having them taught by palace tutors. Charles was the first heir to the throne ever to experience this, but the innovation worked so well that Prince Edward decided he would like to try his hand at teaching leisure activities and games.

Surrounded by her sons

Both the Queen and Prince Philip recognise that
there is more in education than you get out of books.
Prince Philip's Duke of Edinburgh Award Scheme
emphasises fitness and initiative, as well as knowledge
of the countryside. As he puts it, the bookworm and
the gladiator each lead only half a life. Prince
Charles has certainly had a wide training, at school,
university and in the services. But in what counts, he
says he's learnt most the way a monkey learns — by
watching his parents.

In winning form

As a young princess, with her mother, father and sister at Royal Lodge, Windsor

Queen Elizabeth has thus succeeded in carrying the warm family style established by her parents through to her own children, and now to her grandchildren. Prince Charles has emphasised the happiness of their close-knit family life. He and his father have both commented on the sheer necessity in their position of having a sense of humour, and those who know the Queen have found that the dignity of her public presence is balanced by a very real sense of fun, expressed within the family circle.

The emphasis she has chosen to put on the family, not just in private but in public life, has been another thing that has prevented Royalty in Britain from becoming an unreal cardboard symbol that ordinary families could not identify with. No single national figurehead could compete with what Prince Philip has called her "family business", so clearly centred on a real family, with real affections and problems.

From the Queen Mother to the Princess of Wales; from Prince William to Prince Andrew; between them, in all their contrasting ways, they appeal to very different kinds of people.

The Royal Family at Balmoral

We talk of the Soldiers of the Queen and of her Royal Air Force and Royal Navy (each vessel named HMS . . . Her Majesty's Ship); and as the envelopes tell, the Government works 'O.H.M.S.': 'On Her Majesty's Service'. But it is well over two hundred and fifty years since any British monarch over-ruled Parliament. Nowadays, the Royal Family offer a focus for the nation's patriotism, separate from political ambition. In this Constitutional Monarchy, as Charles has said, there isn't any power: any influence they have simply reflects the respect people have for the Royal Family personally. According to the veteran politician Lord George-Brown, this makes a monarchy the best form of Presidency that anyone could invent.

Be that as it may, events such as the Queen's Jubilee, the wedding of her oldest son, and the birth of a grandson continuing the direct line to the throne, are greeted with remarkable warmth of feeling. Pretty clearly, people not only in the United Kingdom and Commonwealth, but in many other parts of the world too, *like* having a Royal Family to represent the nation of Britain . . . a Royal Family shaped through the long reign of a lady who (like her mother) was not actually 'born to be a Queen'.

Family Tree

WILHELMINA CHARLOTTE CAROLINE,
daughter of JOHANN FRIEDRICH,
MARGRAVE of BRANDENBURG-ANSBACH
Married 22nd August 1705
Died 20th November 1737

GEORGE II,
KING of GREAT BRITAIN & IRELAND
Crowned 11th October 1727 in Westminster Abbey
Born 30th October 1683
Died 25th October 1760

AUGUSTA,
daughter of FRIEDRICH II,
DUKE of SAXE-GOTHA-ALTENBURG
Married 8th May 1736
Died 8th February 1772

FREDERICK LOUIS,
PRINCE of WALES and EARL of CHESTER
So created 8th January 1729
Born 20th January 1707
Died 20th March 1751

GEORGE III,
KING of GREAT BRITAIN & IRELAND
Crowned 22nd September 1761 in Westminster Abbey
Born 4th June 1738
Died 29th January 1820

SOPHIA CHARLOTTE,
daughter of KARL LUDWIG FRIEDRICH,
DUKE of MECKLENBURG-STRELITZ
Married 8th September 1761
Died 17th November 1818

VICTORIA MARY LOUISA,
daughter of FRANZ FRIEDRICH ANTON,
DUKE of SAXE-COBURG-SAALFELD
Married 11th July 1818
Died 16th March 1861

EDWARD,
DUKE of KENT & STRATHEARN; so created 24th April 1799
Governor of Gibraltar, 1802-3
Born 2nd November 1767
Died 23rd January 1820